Sign Language & Weather

Bela Davis

Abdo Kids Junior
is an Imprint of Abdo Kids
abdobooks.com

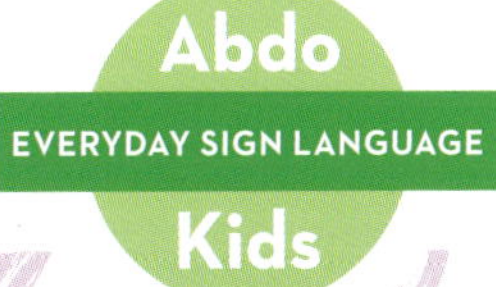

abdobooks.com

Published by Abdo Kids, a division of ABDO, P.O. Box 398166, Minneapolis, Minnesota 55439.

Printed in the United States of America, North Mankato, Minnesota.

102024

012025

THIS BOOK CONTAINS RECYCLED MATERIALS

Photo Credits: Shutterstock

Production Contributors: Teddy Borth, Jennie Forsberg, Grace Hansen

Design Contributors: Candice Keimig, Pakou Moua

Library of Congress Control Number: 2024936609

Publisher's Cataloging-in-Publication Data

Names: Davis, Bela, author.

Title: Sign language & weather / by Bela Davis

Description: Minneapolis, Minnesota : Abdo Kids, 2025 | Series: Everyday sign language set 3 | Includes online resources and index.

Identifiers: ISBN 9798384902812 (lib. bdg.) | ISBN 9798384903512 (ebook) | ISBN 9798384903864 (Read-to-me ebook)

Subjects: LCSH: American Sign Language--Juvenile literature. | Weather--Juvenile literature. | Deaf--Means of communication--Juvenile literature. | Language acquisition--Juvenile literature.

Classification: DDC 419--dc23

Table of Contents

Signs and Weather

ASL is a visual language. There is a sign for all types of weather!

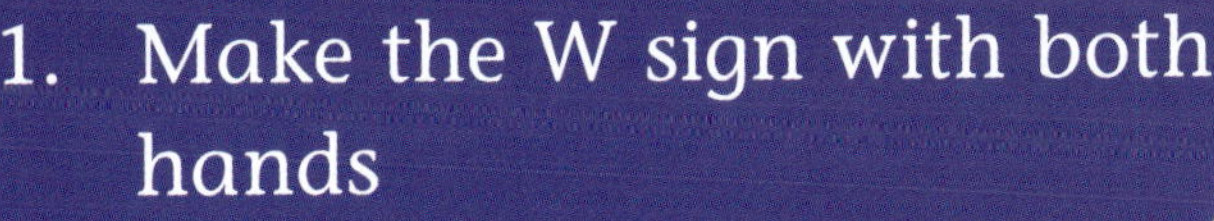

WEATHER

1. Make the W sign with both hands
2. Hold both hands at head height, palms facing out
3. Move both hands down in a wavy motion

The sun is out! Maria needs her sunglasses.

SUN

1. Make a circle with the pointer finger up above the head
2. Then touch the fingers and thumb together and angle them downward toward the face
3. Spread the fingers apart, as if shining a light on the face

Lucas looks up to the sky.

He sees a cloud shaped

like a bear.

CLOUDS

1. Make two open C hands
2. Bring hands up to eye level, with the thumbs and fingers pointed toward each other
3. Move the C hands in and out and around in a circle away from the body
4. It should look like the outline of a fluffy cloud

The rain has not stopped all day. But Teddy still goes outside for a walk.

RAIN

1. Bring open hands up above the head, palms facing down
2. Bend wrists up and down as the hands fall slowly toward the ground
3. It should look like raindrops falling from the sky

Thunder can sound scary.

But Alexa is safe inside.

THUNDER

1. Point to the ear with one hand
2. Then make fists with both hands, bringing them to chest height, and move them from side to side

Thunderstorms make lightning. Lightning can light up a stormy sky.

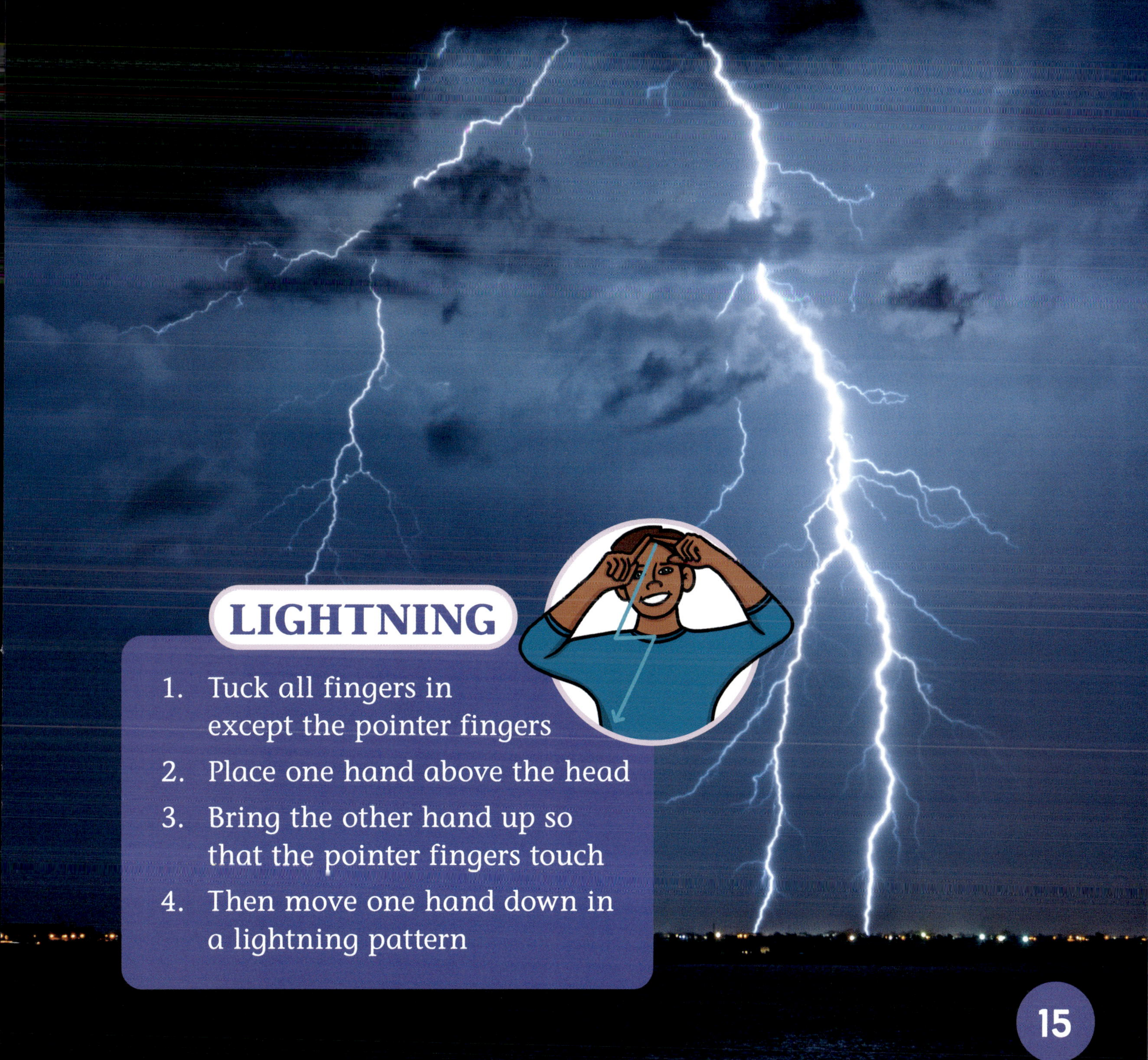

LIGHTNING

1. Tuck all fingers in except the pointer fingers
2. Place one hand above the head
3. Bring the other hand up so that the pointer fingers touch
4. Then move one hand down in a lightning pattern

It's a snow day! James and Mae get to stay home from school.

SNOW

1. Bring both open hands up to head height
2. Bring the hands down slowly while wiggling all the fingers

Tornadoes are common in spring and summer. They can be very **destructive**.

TORNADO

1. Tuck all fingers in except the pointer fingers
2. Place hands in front of the body, one above and one below, and point the pointer fingers toward one another
3. Rotate hands in a spinning motion while widening the gap between them

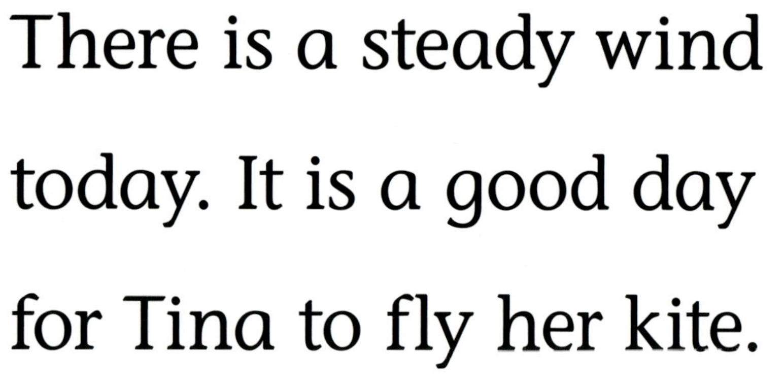

There is a steady wind today. It is a good day for Tina to fly her kite.

WIND

1. Bring both open hands up in front of the body
2. Palms should be facing each other and be several inches apart
3. Move the arms back and forth while keeping the hands parallel

The ASL Alphabet!

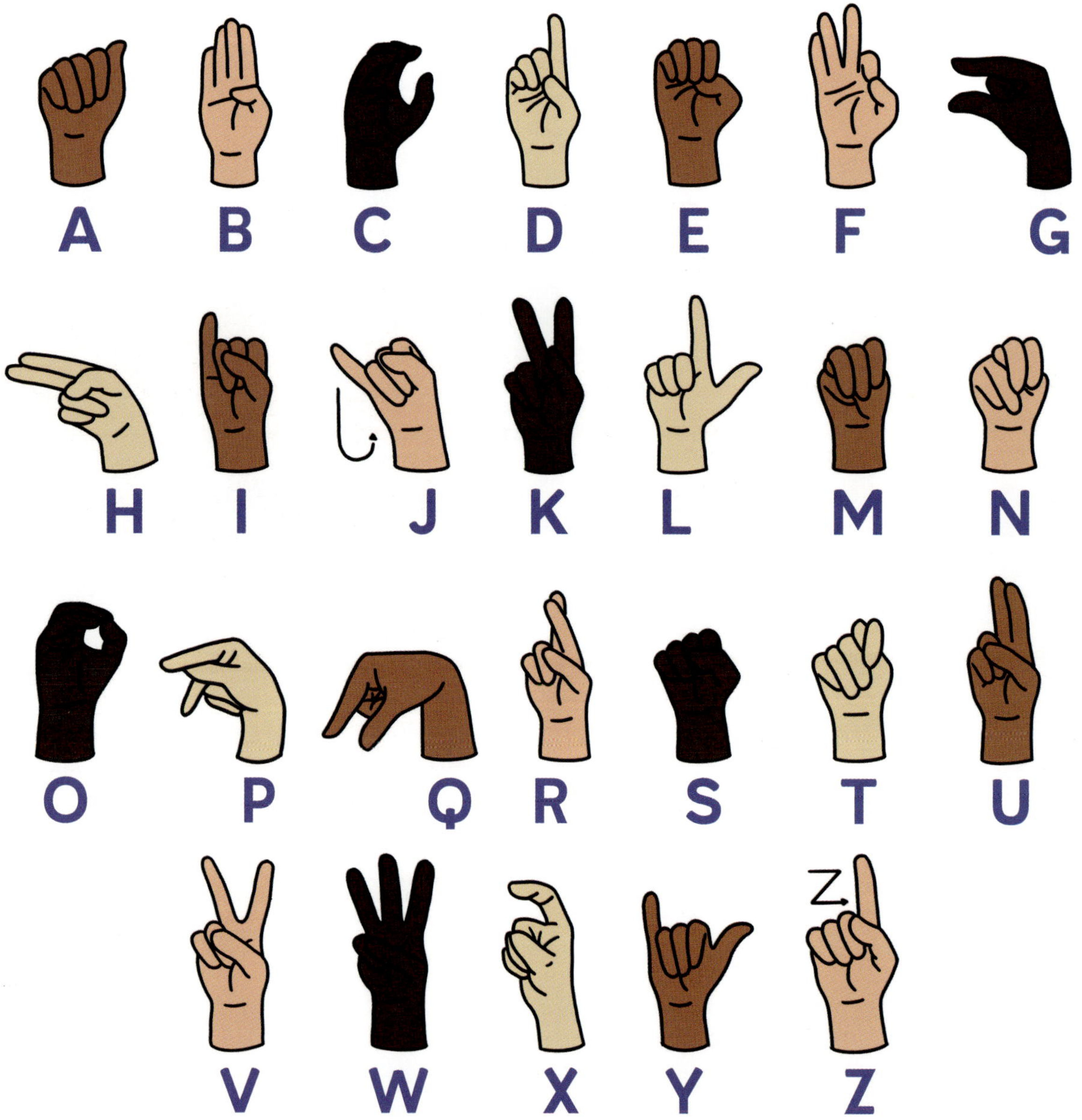

A B C D E F G

H I J K L M N

O P Q R S T U

V W X Y Z

Glossary

ASL
short for American Sign Language, a language used by many deaf people in North America.

destructive
causing complete ruin.

Index

Visit **abdokids.com** to access crafts, games, videos, and more!

Use Abdo Kids code

ESK2812

or scan this QR code!